I0555431

Silent

I feel the wind

cold yet warm

the cool breeze

the thunder storm

your silent voice

patient yet strong

the river flowing

the time unknowing

your silent voice

yes I can hear

the stars disturb me

the air preserves me

here yet gone

through the thunder storm

~Barbara Fergerson~

The Many Moods of a Woman

The Many Moods of a Woman

Copyright© 2026, 2023

Evette T. Fergerson

All rights reserved. No part of this book may be used or reproduced in any manner whatsoever without the written permission of the author.

Edited and Designed by:
Denice D. Richards

Cover artwork designed by:
Victoria Rusyn

Revised Edition

ISBN 979-8-218-13005-3 (paperback)
ISBN 979-8-218-15980-1 (eBook)

Published by IngramSpark

Printed in the United States of America

The Many Moods of a Woman

The Poetic Storytelling of
Evette T. Fergerson

The Ride

· ·

Love

Hurt

Pleasure

Pain

Final Word

Intro

*B*eing a woman is exhausting. At times, it feels like a thankless role, one filled with raw emotion, because we are constantly wearing so many hats.

We are mothers, daughters, friends, lovers, wives, career women, business owners, and creative souls. And sometimes, we are simply everyday women, flawed, evolving, and carrying emotional scars shaped by relationships and life experiences. No matter the season we are in, we often carry the weight of the world on our shoulders, while standing strong, guided by an unspoken inner strength that helps us face the fires of our daily battles.

Life has a way of knocking us down, sometimes repeatedly. In those moments, we can choose to let it defeat us, or we can push through. Often, that choice creates a mental shield, one built layer by layer, that protects the core of who we truly are, much like a rose bud tightly wrapped around its center.

Those layers form the many dimensions of being a woman. As we learn, heal, and grow, those petals begin to loosen and unravel, transforming us into something more open, more powerful, and more beautiful.

These petals, these layers, represent the many moods of a woman. We internalize so much that our reactions often shape how we respond, setting the emotional tone for each moment in time.

The Many Moods of a Woman is a poetic journey of self-discovery. The stories woven throughout these pages reflect our shared experiences with love, hurt, pleasure, and pain, each one honoring the depth of our emotional lives.

We love deeply. We ride hard for the people we care about. Sometimes, we remain in situations we know are unhealthy, choosing to search for the good rather than walking away. Love can be complicated, and at times, it leaves us doubting our worth and questioning whether we deserve the love we seek.

Yet even in hurt, we rise.

We are wounded, and still, we bounce back, stronger, wiser, and more resilient each time.

When we learn to love ourselves first, pleasure takes on a new meaning. Self-love creates an indescribable euphoria, one so powerful that it can sometimes be mistaken for love itself, when in truth, it is a fantasy playing out within our own minds.

Motherhood, however, elevates love to an entirely different level. It reshapes how we think, how we feel, and how we see the world. Through it, our love for ourselves deepens, and our perspective on people and life shifts forever.

We also experience pain through relationships and society's expectations, through the way others see us and, at times, treat us. Yet within that pain exists balance. When love, hurt, pleasure, and pain intersect, they give our lives meaning and depth.

Through every adversity we face, we continue to rise, celebrating the true essence of womanhood and honoring our victories as we overcome our tragedies.

I hope you enjoy this emotional roller coaster ride as much as I enjoyed writing it.

Welcome to *The Many Moods of a Woman.*

Love

Our Song

We are women and we are smart,
talented, independent, and fabulous.
We make remarkable things happen,
when we're multi-tasking.
We set goals and achieve them.
Honor our parents and believe them
when they say we are winners in their eyes
and don't forget, baby girl, you're the prize.
Walk with your head held high,
and be wise, making decisions in life.
We are women.
At times, we're complicated
or misbehavin'
depending on the day or date shall I say.
We are amazing in our own way.
We step up to the plate
and make the impossible possible.
For without us the world wouldn't populate
due to our ovulation chart.
We are women and we are brave.
To our men: don't be afraid if we're too strong.
We had to be through history
when others did us wrong.
But, if you're patient you'll see,
our love runs deep, as deep can be,
and we'll treat you like a king on a throne,

4 ⁓

standing beside you
like the queen we were born to be.
And trust, we'll show you nothing but loyalty.
We are women who wear many hats.
We are mothers who'll protect our children
no matter what.
Wives who stand by our husband's side.
Sisters who will ride or die.
We're cousins, granddaughters,
friends to the end,
and great lovers.
We run companies and have our own businesses,
while some of us are just everyday women,
hustling, trying to get ahead of the game,
making it all look easy.
With various styles on our heads –
naturally curly, kinky, blowed out, or pressed,
short cuts, dreadlocks, wigs, braided, or weaved up – our
morning hair mess is our crown and glory.
And yes, we are blessed beyond this story,
with our stilettos on and a smile on our face,
keeping our families happy
or our single life in place.
We are women, hear me now.
We live out loud
and we are proud
to be exactly who we were created to be.
We are royalty to the Most-High.
And oh yes, everyone knows we are fly,
or else the media wouldn't glorify the things we've had

The Many Moods of a Woman

our entire lives.
We are women with beautiful thighs,
luscious lips, and seductive eyes,
and we're not all just one size.
We thrive on being the women we are.
We are women,
and this is *Our Song.*

To My Darling Zoë

Happy Birthday!
December 27, 2013
5:42 a.m.

My Dearest Zoë:
With beautiful brown eyes
twinkling like stars in the sky,
You are my precious gift from God, The Most High.
There are no words to describe
the overwhelming love I feel for you.
Thank you for choosing me to be born through.
I gave you life, and you, too, gave me life.
How could I possibly split this love if I had two?
However, I know it's possible,
because many mommies do.
But for now, my little angel face, it's just you and I.
I cannot begin to tell you how you've changed my life.
Made me more sensitive to other human beings.
Slowed me down and made me see
things differently.
Through a brand-new set of eyes,
living life for a second time.
You're amazing!
And you amaze me everyday.
I love how we play,
spend time reading books,

The Many Moods of a Woman

running around dancing,
making funny faces,
falling out laughing.
Your laughter is like music to my ears.
Your smile brings me to tears.
Reliving the moment
you were growing inside of me, my dear.
I can clearly hear your heartbeat and
I feel your little feet kicking me.
I feel you moving constantly.
What an exciting feeling of life
growing inside of me.
My love was unconditional
from the moment you were conceived.
My darling Zoë,
you are a gift from God sent to me,
and I believe you were only meant for me.
What a beautiful, incredible, forever blessing.
I had to think of a name befitting of you.
With "LIFE" as its meaning,
I chose ZOË for you.
How beautiful!
You also have two middle names,
orchestrated by your father and I,
because we couldn't decide.
He loved Essence, but Harper was my choice.
Zoë Essence Harper
was wonderfully designed by us both.
Thank you for being such a beautiful soul.
You are smart, great, and bold.
God's masterpiece.

A beautiful gift created only for me.
My wish came true with you.
I promise to always protect you,
guide you,
support your dreams,
stand beside you.
I may make mistakes along the way,
but know my intentions for you are always great.
To provide the best for you,
an unconditional love so true.
I'll always speak highly of you,
and speak greatness upon you.
As we maneuver through life side by side,
I know one day my little birdie will have to fly.
And I pray I've prepared you to soar through life,
reach the sky and climb new heights.
Achieve all your dreams, stay focused, and bright.
Have fun along the way,
always make time to play.
Make God a part of your every day.
And the decisions you make for yourself,
whether wrong or right,
are lessons learned,
not mistakes in life.
You will have failures, but hold your head high.
Keep the drive.
Through those failures
out comes a beautiful surprise
of achieving your highest goals in life.
And you can do it because I believe in you.

The Many Moods of a Woman

Your father believes in you.
Remember, you can do
whatever you set your mind to.
You are smart.
You are bold and beautiful.
You are the prize and you are wise
beyond your years.
You have a big heart.
You are fearless.
You live life with no glass ceiling.
You enjoy being who you are.
You are valued.
You are a precious jewel,
a diamond whose personality shines so bright.
Never dim your light.
Greatness lives within you.
Nobody's words can ever hurt you.
Your father and I adore you.
No one is above you.
We love you!
And when choosing the love of your life,
make sure he's right for you,
has pure love so true.
Just as pure as the unconditional love
we have shown you.
Never mistreating you, only blessings continued.
These are my wishes for you.
My Life.
My Love.
My Zoë Bug!
Forever unconditional love, Mommy!

One Day

As I sit here staring at my computer screen,
I dream of meeting you one day in an
unconventional way my friend,
who is a true gentleman.
You're interesting to me
because our conversations are unique.
You keep me intrigued, by the way you think.
Your musical taste is all over the place
– just like mine.
It's the way we unwind,
act silly, sing songs, and just vibe.
At times, I speak and you finish my sentences.
You're my guy and I feel alive when we
look at each other knowing we have a secret code.
Our own language.
Our love language.
At times, it's strange to others
how we connected as friends,
but are now lovers.
You are my Lover,
my Friend,
my Gentleman.
As I lay here and look in your eyes, I
feel protected – as I should.
You're protective over me.
Not in a bad way, but in a great way.

The Many Moods of a Woman

You understand your duties as a man,
to protect and provide and do the best you can
for your family.
You're also true to me.
Oh how I love your loyalty.
Our relationship means everything,
and others who try us will know
that you don't play when it comes to you and I.
You sing our praises to the most high,
praying for our unity, future, and family.
We both have a spiritual mind.
You're my #1 guy and one day, I'll be inclined to tell you
how I prayed for you to come my way,
to meet me in an unconventional way
my Friend,
my Gentleman,
my Lover.
One day, you'll be my husband.
I know this to be true,
because the universe has brought me to you.
So, I stay still until the day you are ready
to open your eyes and receive your prize,
your future,
your wife.
I'm not chasing you because that's not for me to do,
but for you to do when you realize
your future is now in front of you.
The minute you take your blinders off
and are whole heartedly ready to accept me, us, we,
you'll know I'm the One.

And I'll be ready to receive you my Friend,
my Gentleman,
my Lover.
And one day you'll be my husband.
Yes, one day you'll be my husband.
My husband!

A Letter To Our Black Men

Dear Black Men:

My heart pours out to you because there's nothing you can do to be safe in a place where we're all supposed to be FREE!

At times, I'm scared for you – and me. It's as if they want to turn back history and try, in their little minds, to put us back in our "so called" place.

You see, they're intimidated because we are Kings and Queens, and it seems the more powerful we become – taking back our pride and then some – the more cowardly they become.

They shoot up our men and our daughters like a badge of honor, and this troubles me to see innocent people killed, and they're all Black – like me.

There's no solid reason for them being buried 6-feet under. My heart is grieving for their crying mothers and families.

How ironic these are all cop killings. I'm starting to think there is a conspiracy theory against our men and women's children, to emasculate them and make them feel less than.

Make them feel they can't walk down the street, or get pulled over by a cop without fear of being shot!

My people, this has to stop! Wake up!

Yet, you want to know why we're described and categorized as angry individuals. Take a look at our history and please tell me, how would you feel if you were constantly targeted like animals in a hunting field?

Black Men, hear me now! Continue to shine your light! Stand tall and proud, and play it smart when dealing with the good ol' boys in blue who's supposed to be there to protect and serve you.

Black Men, know that we stand beside you, with our fist held high exuding Black Pride!

We are proud of you and we love you.

They are not above you.

We are all equal.

Wake up my people!

From Your First True Love,
A Black Woman

The Many Moods of a Woman

My Sistas

As women, we feel the weight of the world on our shoulders. For Black women, that weight gets 10 times heavier – like metal boulders.

As I get older, I realize my tolerance level is on zero regarding the negative stereotypical imagery concerning my people, especially our everyday Shero's.

Black women, who are often misrepresented and tend to be the forgotten ones (even though we gave birth to this entire nation).

We are strong to the core, built from the beginning more resilient than any other human being.

If you don't believe me, check the statistical facts of what I'm saying. Black women were born to thrive in a world where the odds are stacked up against us time after time.

In us we trust, running circles around our counterparts we must, yet still not getting the accolades that are deserving of us.

We work 10 times harder just to prove ourselves and to be seen as equal partners to everyone else.

But, we are not equal; what we do is devalued as if we don't matter at all.

Others look at us with a smile but secretly hope we fall.

Constantly torn down, spirits shattered, and still, we break down walls.

We get up, dust ourselves off, and push harder, being more strategic in our movements, studying, and getting smarter.

How sad to know you feel threatened by me.

Most days I walk this Earth in disbelief when others try and devalue our worth. But we are worthy!

Our contributions to the world are often overlooked and overshadowed by the arrogance and ignorance of those who can't believe how savvy we truly are.

But we're changing the game now!

Sistas, put on your crown, shoulders back, chin up.

Stand your ground and walk proud.

Know that you are a Queen.

Holding yourselves to higher standards, walking the walk like no one better.

You are fierce, a woman who many dream to be, with natural beauty, flawless skin, and impeccable style that sets trends.

You are a true woman of dignity, who is brave and often enslaved in society's depiction of who they want us to be, instead of who we are naturally.

We are strong beyond their words or comprehension.

They can't hold us down because our resilience is from another dimension.

You are worthy of love and all the great things life brings you. Never mind how everyone else sees you because you are the light and the epitome of unconditional love.

So, don't think twice about the goals you have in mind for yourself; you've been brainwashed to self-sabotage, to throw you off track.

Don't sweat it and keep going my Sistas, because God's got your back.

Soul Connection

You and I have this euphoric vibe,
our energy intertwined with our souls,
making our connection bold.
I feel free to reveal my inner thoughts to you,
knowing I'm safe
because you feel the same way I do.
I trust you.
We connect on another level,
and you're free to be yourself around me.
Free to love openly.
Free to trust me to hold your secrets deep within,
with no judgment attached, love showered.
I got your back.
You're my friend first, before my lover,
and our connection is deeper than any other.
This soul connection
has us rejecting outside negativity.
The universe chose you for me.
Our world is us, cosmically.
You're my muse, and I know I'm yours, too.
We inspire each other's poetic truths.
We hold each other accountable to a fault,
and your thought process is amazing.
I love the way you think and converse with me.
You're my happy place.

Sometimes, it's a mystery of why we click so perfectly,
but I won't question it.
Enjoy our special place
my friend.
My muse.
My you.
A soul connection so true.

Love Joy

You've changed me in ways no one ever has.
With you, I'm open.
With you, I'm honestly me,
transparent, wholeheartedly.
My being outspoken is never a challenge for you,
and you appreciate me for who I am.
We fit within this comfortable groove,
and I adore you.
Being me has never been more freeing
than being with you.
Slowly peeling back the layers of life,
learning the history between us two,
our unspoken truth.
With you, I'm healing
one dysfunction at a time,
and growing in tremendous strides.
With you by my side,
not judging me for a moment,
embracing my flaws.
I'm loving every minute
of getting to know you all over again.
Taking it back to when we first dated,
excitement on 10!
Once my close friend,
you're now much more than I've ever imagined us to be.
Feelings of butterflies fluttering,

what is this feeling that runs so deep?
Thank you for not giving up on me.
On us.
Knowing what you wanted,
staying focused and determined.
At times, thinking of giving up.
But you didn't.
Patience was key,
now we're moving in the direction
of our life goals and dreams.
You're my King and I'm your Queen,
sitting on the throne raising our princesses, 1-2-3,
to walk proudly into their own destiny.
I love how we look at each other
and the way in which we speak,
laying our cards on the table.
Your curiosity runs deep,
asking the hard questions
that were never answered before.
Learning us to the next level
with kindness and genuine trust,
building a mental fortress
around what we've created between us.
Breaking down walls,
fiercely protecting our legacy.
Us.
Following our core values,
in one God we trust.
Uniquely made for each other,
we formed a bond like no other,

creating a new chapter together.
This is our time beyond measure,
with infinite pleasure.
Our story, Love Joy
has taken over.
Forever.

I Don't Apologize

I don't apologize for the way I live my life
in anyone's eyes.
I am who I am, and I'm me with pride.
I don't apologize for being direct
and honest with who I am.
The mistakes you may see
are learning lessons for me.
I'm not perfect by far.
I have many flaws and emotional scars
which I've released.
Living the life of no apologies.
I don't apologize for who I am.
Yes, I've been married twice.
Had a taste of the good life.
Working with superstars.
Having affairs,
and driving fast cars.
At times, spiraling out of control
but I was able to dig myself out of that hole.
I'm living the life I want to live,
with no fear!
Taking chances and being clear about my choices,
the ones I've made for only me.
The choices I've made, with no apologies.
I don't apologize for being open-minded
and curious at times,

testing my boundaries, living on the edge.
Jumping out of planes,
and making my own rules
in this school called life.
But don't get it twisted,
at times, I think twice.
But I don't apologize for being me:
ambitious, creative, and at times a mystery.
But free to express myself
without biting my tongue.
Don't dish it out if you can't take it, son!
I am controlling at times, and I am bold.
I've taken care of myself since I was 18 years old.
Pushed from the nest with wings to fly,
my parents gave me the tools I needed to survive,
and I'm still alive.
Thank God for that!
I'm still focused and driven to thrive.
I don't apologize for being who I am.
I want more; no ordinary life for me,
or else I'll get bored.
And that is my number one enemy.
There are so many layers to who you see.
I'm loyal in relationships,
but when single, I'm free.
I'm your friend to the end,
no mistake about it,
but when I'm crossed,
I'll build a wall that's solid.

The Many Moods of a Woman

I don't apologize for being me,
or for the way I live my life in anyone's eyes.
I am who I am.
I'm me with pride.
And for that
I don't apologize.

Hurt

Back Pocket Guy

Back Pocket Guy, help me understand why
you crept back into my life,
making me think twice about my relationship?
We had something a while ago,
and at times you came back
to see if what we had would fly.
Well, we can't fly if you're still tied down.
Haven't you realized that by now?
So tell me, why are you here?
Trying to tempt me
to do what you wouldn't want me to
if I was with you.
Your job, I see, is to test me.
Making a mess of things
while talking sweet nothings in my ear.
I see you over there with your significant other,
telling me how she's a bother,
and you're not happy
because of one thing or another.
And yet, you haven't left her.
Please stop!
When you're unhappy, you come to me,
to feel free,
to see if the grass is greener.
Well, it's not!
That is, not for you.

I'm not here to be your fall back girl
just because you're mad at your boo.
I'm tired of us playing this game,
going back and forth, doing the same thing
and getting the same result.
Absolutely nothing!
Back, Pocket Guy.
I know it's hard to leave us behind
and leave well enough alone,
because we've known each other for so long.
We had electrifying chemistry
but never pursued it entirely,
which is why you keep trying.
And our chapter seems incomplete
because there's something about us
that's intriguing to you.
But we'll never find out
if you don't approach me with a clean slate,
to see if what we have or had is true,
or would one day be great!
Deep down, we both know it will never be.
I know we have history,
had all the time in the world
to find out what we could have been,
yet something still keeps us here
in this incomplete hemisphere.
Now, think wise.
You have someone in front of you
who seems meant for you.
Who you've pursued.

Who you've moved in with.
Building memories and having big dreams with.
Yet, you have the nerve to ask why we're not one?
Come on, son!
I'm not the one.
Because we never pursued it to be
you and me,
and the reality is, it will never be.
I had to come to grips with that
and stop living a fantasy from way back.
So, I release you
to be who you are supposed to be with,
which isn't me, as you see.
Now, Back Pocket Guy,
you're where you need to be.
Which is behind me,
zipped in the back pocket of our false reality.
And now, we're both free,
and can reflect on our history
as just a fond memory.

Rose Colored Glasses

He was supposed to be the love of my life,
but mistakenly, I was unable to recognize this guy
who showed me his true side.
You see,
I thought he was different from all the rest.
With us living together,
what a disappointing hot mess.
To find out he was much worse
than I anticipated.
This scorned love story is truly complicated.
Was this really who I thought
was supposed to be "The One?"
Thinking to myself,
"God, why are you playing this cruel joke on me?"
As I reflect on what should have been,
I had to check myself and look deep within.
This love story was supposed to thrive
through the end of time.
Step back a moment.
Now breathe.
God had nothing to do with it.
This was all my creative ruin.
This guy was just being himself unapologetically,
while I turned a blind eye.
Pursuing him
with rose colored glasses on, pathetically.

Not paying attention to any of the signs,
that were right in front of my eyes.
Only seeing what I wanted to see,
what I imagined for so many years.
Crushing on him as a teen,
not knowing his full story about who he was.
Only believing the dream
I romanticized in my head,
a fantasy so strong it misled me.
I stayed in this toxic-ship,
thinking things were going to change,
but of course, it made a turn for the worse,
time and time again like a bad script unrehearsed.
The love of my life,
in my eyes and mind, was a go-getter,
driven to succeed beyond measure.
He was kind, generous, and a lover of life.
Not in a million years
I wouldn't have thought twice
when it came to him and I.
After all, he was supposed to have been my life.
So, I had to analyze the situation.
Pulling back the layers with aggravated hesitation.
Is the person I really see,
a true reflection of me?
No. No, it couldn't be.
See, I set out and go after what I want to achieve.
No idle dreams.
And if there's pain inside,
my soul can't hide or disguise it.

Walking around with a happy grin or smiling face,
only if that pain is erased.
See, this person – the love of my life –
who I thought one day would be,
cannot possibly be a reflection of me.
But there is a reason why he chose me.
Could it be he picked up on how I self-sabotage
my pitiful-self,
deep down not believing
I am deserving of true love,
and doubting myself?
Am I the one holding my heart back
from what I truly deserve?
Smothering my love dreams
with thoughts unseen,
deeply rooted in pain
of not thinking I'm enough.
Covering it up with one too many bad decisions.
Calculating my own selfish needs.
Hunting the next victim of my love schemes,
leaving behind too many casualties.
So yes,
perhaps I was a reflection of who he really was.
He was crippled in life,
while I was crippled in love.

This Guy

Candles burning on my nightstand,
I hear a knock at my door.
Lean over to look at my watch.
It's one o'clock in the morning.
I am not going to the door.
Whoever it is must have the wrong floor.
Then, my phone rings.
I pick up.
He says,
"Hi, it's me."
I think to myself, "He must be crazy!"
Coming to my door at one o'clock in the morning,
as if I have no other lovers.
OK, I don't,
but that's beside the point.
I open the door to his smiling face.
We embrace.
His voice makes me moist.
I look at him and say,
"What are you doing here, man?"
He replied,
"I heard you needed some fun in your life,"
then pulled out a little baggy of purple haze.
Within the hour, we were blazed.
Floating on a cloud, deep in conversation.

Being creative and wise,
watching the room come alive.
At the time
even my little dog was on cloud nine.
Then, our eyes met.
He blew smoke into my mouth.
Shotgun one.
Then shotgun number two.
When he touched me,
each touch seemed brand new,
as if he'd never felt me before.
The intensity made my body cry.
This guy!
Creeping like a thief in the night.
He started kissing me passionately.
Turning me around,
finding the hot spot
on the back of my neck.
He's caressing me with his fingers down below,
real slow.
Before I knew it,
his two fingers entered my shaved hole.
Trying to find the wet road on "G" Street,
I moaned.
Each time was so different from the rest.
Our bodies sweaty on the floor,
right next to my French doors.
With sensual sounds playing in the background,
his hands came from behind
to caress my breast now.

The Many Moods of a Woman

His hardness entered me slowly
where the road wet from rain flowed.
He held me around my waist,
going deeper into my sweet place.
Until I cried, tears flowing from my eyes.
Oh damn!
This guy!
I arched my back to take him all in.
The feeling was electrifying.
Oh yes!
I'm still crying,
and he feels AMAZING!
I never know what to expect from this guy,
but he always leaves me satisfied.
Why can't he be mine, full-time?
Then he turns me around.
Spreads my legs wide,
as if I were a butterfly.
And we came
simultaneously in flight.
Oh yes!
This guy!
I'm still crying on the inside.
Tears flowing
as we collapse on my living room floor.
Looking into each other's eyes,
I'm knowing,
our souls once again intertwined.
Crying on the inside.
This guy!

38 ~

Why can't he be mine?
Oh my.
Why can't he be mine?

Me First

He's married.
But, according to his voice, on the verge of divorce.
Out of the house, but still back and forth.
I was a fool to open my heart to you,
I bent my rules for a moment or two.
We vibe with each other on another level,
getting closer over time, building on ideas together,
loving up on each other.
You said you were through.
I believed you.
So open and vulnerable.
Through your eyes, I saw our lives intertwined,
yet you're still unavailable.
This is unbearable.
Each day that we grow closer,
I can't help but feel anxious.
Is it me as his lover?
Or does he still love her?
I'm sick of being in the shadows,
rearranging my life to fit into your ideal schedule.
I'm sick of being hurt,
and yet you want me to be patient?
I'm sick of being the cool chick,
without limitations.
No more, I can't take it!
I'm sick of the waiting game.

But I don't blame you,
you're only doing what I allowed you to.
Now I'm tired of this thing we have together.
I know you're loving us, but it's not enough for me.
My heart is on the line.
I need to pull it together.
The reality is, I deserve so much better.
It's time to take my power back.
No unnecessary pressure,
just get your life together!
Today and always, I put myself first.
Today is the day for the shift, unrehearsed.
Allow myself to grow
with someone who's fully available to me.
Knowing beyond a doubt,
I am worthy of being happy.
Being true to myself,
I love myself more than I love you.
I've listened for months, still singing that old tune.
And the broken record continues.
This is not how I pictured my future to be,
with someone who can't even
move forward with me.
And show up for me.
And protect me,
when I haven't even shown up for myself.
Protecting my heart from an unavailable fantasy.
Today, I break this situational curse,
choosing my happiness and choosing me first.

The Many Moods of a Woman

Pleasure

Dark Bourbon

He was the smoothest man I've ever known.
Embracing me with hugs,
welcoming me back home.
Bald head, grown beard, stylish
with a baritone voice in my ear.
Sipping dark bourbon,
his intentions were clear.
Deep brown eyes looking deeply into mine.
Perking up my soul, awakening my sensual side.
Paired with his touch
those eyes ignite the sensual sexy vibes.
Our attraction is magnetized times five.
I'm alive, with his sensitizing, energetic,
stimulating, non-competitive mental ride.
Damn, He's FINE!
I sit back and take a sip of my red wine
as I watch him undress me
with his hypnotizing brown eyes.
Slow dancing,
we're in tune as he softly caresses my thigh.
I want him more than ever before.
He's a bit arrogant knowing I'm into him,
just as much as he's into me.
Not wanting to disclose his true feelings
because of our history.

Oh, but I know his inner desires are for us to be
intertwined in the most passionate hold,
romantically embracing.
The thought of our foreplay.
Hearts racing!
His lips to my lips,
kissing passionately.
Slight tickle to my chin
from his beard's masculinity.
Exploring every inch of my body,
and I'm mentally drowning
in his lustful seductive mind state.
This man truly takes my breath away.
Our connection is so powerful
that it ignites the fire we both desire.
With us, the level of intensity
goes beyond anyone's comprehension.
His stroke is so powerful,
filling every dimension of my lady flower.
Fitting like a glove
it sensationally rubs against my wall showers.
I holler, "Yes, baby!
Oh, right there, don't stop!
Please go deeper, deeper, oooohhhhh yessss!!!"
Shit felt so good, it almost made me call my mama.
Sweat dripping from his face to my face.
Soft kisses as we lay and exchange smiles.
Both thinking, "WOW, that was amazing!"
Wait, did I say that out loud?

The Many Moods of a Woman

He rolls off me ever so gently,
lying on his back now,
staring at the ceiling.
Laughing and playing with each other out loud.
I close my eyes while intensely listening
to the harmonic melodies
serenading from his juicy, soft lips.
So beautiful and effortless.
He's in the moment
not realizing just how sexy he is.
So I sit back, smile, and enjoy it.
Close my eyes once again.
Exhale, breathe in.
No way to ignore the orgasmic synergy
of pulsating energy we've just explored.

46 —
Slow Dance

We're having a funky time
listening to tunes by Charlie Parker
and Etta James.
Sitting out on the balcony
overlooking the city skyline.
A romantic setting with just him and I.
As we admire a clear view of the city,
light wind touches my skin, embracing me.
He says I look pretty.
We're reciting poetry and discussing history.
He walks right by my side,
giving each other the eye.
For I am in awe with him
being so intellectual and musical.
He plays me jazz songs,
big bands from decades ago.
Highlighting the greats like
Duke Ellington,
Billie Holiday,
John Coltrane,
and occasionally
Quincy Jones.
As we puff, puff smoke, I choke.
He laughs at me,
thinking it's cute and funny.

I'm high from the trees he has given me,
while we study the relaxed, romantic melodies.
He is unique, and I love that about him.
Has a strong demeanor.
A real man,
no doubt about it.
He showers me with affection.
He moves his hand to massage my neck
and rubs my back.
With him, I'm relaxed.
He pours me coconut rum on ice.
With those smokey brown eyes,
he looks me over once or twice.
Takes my hand and leads me to the next room,
slow dancing to another jazz tune
like Sarah Vaughn,
Miles Davis,
and Nina Simone.
Candles strategically placed
all around the room,
the aroma of passion fruit
dancing in the air.
I'm over the moon
as he gently touches my hair.
We look into each other's eyes,
catching a glimpse of our souls colliding.
The room becomes silent,
yet I hear the candlelight flames
flickering in the background.

My mind wanders
as we sit on the sofa connecting,
I want him for my lover.
He pulls me over.
We kiss passionately.
The next thing I know, my clothes are off,
thrown on the floor right next to me.
He admires my body.
Looking at me with those smoky brown eyes,
taking his time,
while he sets the mood with another tune.
This time it's Donny Hathaway.
He takes off his shirt and looks me over.
As he pulls down his pants,
my heart beats like thunder.
He moves towards me real slow,
starts licking every inch of my body
from head to toe.
His hands, examining my pussy flow,
took his tongue and licked my pussy slow.
This intensity is what I yearned for below.
He sits up and I straddle him,
arching my back to ride him,
feeling every bit of his stiffness,
as I'm slowly grinding him.
I feel his full lips kissing my shoulder.
So sweet and tender, he turns me over.
He bends over and pulls my hair
to get in deep, so deep in there.
I don't care about the noises I'm making,

The Many Moods of a Woman

I'm in heaven with his lovemaking.
Our bodies sweaty, glistening from the heat,
he lies on my back, rocking me to sleep.
Slow and electrifying.
Still rocking, going deep.
Music's dying,
I still hear the melodies in my head
of funky jazz tunes and big bands.
We're falling asleep now.
I'm dreaming of slow dancing
in the middle of the room
to Charlie Parker,
Etta James,
Duke Ellington,
Billie Holiday,
John Coltrane,
Quincy Jones,
Sarah Vaughn,
Miles Davis,
Nina Simone, and
Donny Hathaway.
Each tune plays louder than the other,
slowly turning down.
As the candle's flame blows out,
the smoke dances before evaporating.
Lights out,
our breaths in sync.
Now, we're deep asleep.

Cosmic Energy

Your energy makes me wet
every time I think of you.
Wanting you to do the nasty things we do
when I'm alone with you in a room,
or outside in the sunlight.
It doesn't matter.
Our energy is always right.
Which may be wrong for us,
since you're not mine.
I've tried to break it off plenty of times,
but you continue to be my kryptonite,
making me weak at first sight.
You have this control over me,
knowing my body thoroughly
as if it was your own.
Our energy is connected to our souls,
like we were meant to be.
But ironically,
you're with someone else constantly.
At times, I may be as well,
but that doesn't matter,
because I can't stop yearning for you,
and you can't stop wanting me.
We've tried many times before,
even moved thousands of miles away,
but it just makes us want each other even more.

The Many Moods of a Woman

Here you come again,
knock, knocking at my front door.
We've explored so many things over the years,
like our fierce, sexual cosmic hemisphere.
We're upfront and blunt
when it comes to what we want,
and I can't front,
you're exciting to be around.
Not sure if that's connected
to the way you put it down.
You are my drug of choice,
and I'm an addict when it comes to you.
I mistake it for love,
but I know it's 100% lust
that we have for each other
except for us, it's 50 times stronger.
Our animal magnetism gives me the shivers.
As I think about your strong thrusts,
I quiver.
Please step away from me,
I need to breathe.
Our energy makes me weak at the knees.
But we can't keep going down this road
of sexual embrace,
because one day it will all unfold
and explode in our face.
Let's leave well enough alone
and leave this affair without a trace.
Let's walk away with a clean slate,
before something enormous drops on our plate,

like something we can't erase
or call a mistake.
Because regardless,
I do have much love for you,
and I only want the best for us.
Let's stop playing with fire
before the fire smoke chokes us both.
So now, we'll call this romantic affair
a blast from our past
and reminisce on the memories we've had,
instead of the sexual chemistry,
which can turn into our worst enemy.
Please concentrate on you over there,
and I'll concentrate on myself.
Let's agree not to see each other again
in this capacity,
or else we'll both have to pay the hefty price
of changing other lives in this way.
Let's be smart and think.
Is our energy,
sexual chemistry,
animalistic feeling
worth making the mistake
of creating unforgiving heartache?

Car Ride

I took a car ride with my guy,
and I was feeling high.
It was night time.
I had him pull to the side
on a neighborhood street.
We jump in the backseat,
the windows already so steamy
you couldn't even see
how he had me in between the two front seats,
pounding me from behind.
He then turns me on my backside
taking me for another ride.
My legs wrapped around his hips,
my head hitting the gear shift,
car rocking in mischief.
Our hearts pounding so loud,
we couldn't hear the other cars surrounding us,
or knocks on the window.
Oh no, it's the cops!
I roll down the window,
with a devious smile on my face.
"Hello officer."
He looks in with his flashlight,
seeing we're half-dressed,
our clothes a mess.

54 ～

He says,
"Is everything alright?"
"Oh yes, sir, we're fine.
My husband and I had a break from the kids
and we were just talking."
He looks at me, shakes his head,
and says,
"It must have been a deep conversation,
and I'm well aware of these situations.
You guys be safe and try not to stay too late."
"Thanks officer."
I rolled up the window.
We laugh a little,
looking at each other
and our animal magnetism again takes over.
I jump on his lap,
he screwed me to the moon and back.
Then we collapse in the car,
waking up
not knowing where we are.

The Many Moods of a Woman

3 a.m. (Part 1)

One night at a party, our eyes locked.
We're outside on a balcony overlooking the stars.
He was the last one I expected by far,
but he made his intentions known to me
as he passed right behind me
rubbing his manhood against my backside.
At that moment the sexual tension aroused me.
I played shy, but the chemistry was on high.
I never met a guy so bold as he.
In public.
At a party.
Rubbing up against me.
I was turned on by his manly charm,
and he knew it.
He made the advance and I played right into it.
That damn tequila!
What the hell am I doing?
He passed by again,
turning around and giving me the eye.
I followed
as if I'd been hypnotized.
But the party wasn't over.
We had about an hour.
Anxiously waiting
as we played cat and mouse.

My friends are talking,
but I barely hear their voices.
Starring in my own movie now,
moving in slow motion.
Will I make the right choices?
As time goes by,
I feel the heat rise.
Oh boy!
There's going to be trouble with this guy.
At 3 a.m., we all say our goodbyes.
Oh my,
how time flies.
He's talking to his friend outside,
his slanted devilish eyes
looking in my direction
with a smirk on his face.
I asked him, "Do you want a ride?"
He replied, "Of course."
Then he took me for a ride.
We jumped in my jeep,
his head went between my thighs.
Pulling my panties to the side
his tongue found its way to my waterfall.
As I'm trying to concentrate,
driving him home.
Thank God he lives just around the corner.
I pull over.
He invited me upstairs.
Do I dare?
Oh, hell yeah!

The Many Moods of a Woman

He looked at me,
took my hand
and lead me upstairs to his promised land.

Doorway (Part 2)

Tic Toc.
Tic Toc.
I can hear his watch.
It's louder than usual.
Thump, thump goes my heart,
leading me upstairs to his promised land.
I'm trying to understand
the vibe I have with this guy.
An animal magnetism,
that's indescribable.
Why?
Well ... no time to think about it.
He opens the door,
my handbag hits the floor.
He starts kissing me, extremely passionately.
And man, I want more!
Oh yes, I want more!
He pulls me down the hallway
into the doorway.
Next thing I know,
my back was against one side of the post,
supporting my legs,
up high on the other side.
Yes Lawd!
We're doing the most.
Had me doing things I didn't know I could do.

But he knew,
or tried something new with me.
In that moment
he proceeded to have a treat,
and that treat was me.
Elevated in the air, not scared.
wishing there was a camera here,
just to catch this moment in action.
At this point,
I'm not sure if he's packin' down there.
At this point,
I don't care.
Right now, we're in a moment of passion.
As he squeezes my ass
the heat inside me rises.
With each tongue thrust
in between my thighs and,
Oh God, the intensity is so high!
Things are moving in slow motion,
between the doorway,
rocking my ocean.
Next thing I know,
I'm lying on his bed,
looking down, seeing the top of his head,
doing things to me I didn't know he could do.
Thinking to myself,
"Is he the one, or are we just having fun?"
My eyes roll back.
Oh man! Here comes another one!
I start shaking uncontrollably.

60 ～

He stops
to look at me.
Gliding on top,
licking his lips with his tongue.
"Oh please," I beg, "Don't stop!"
He looks my way with that smirk on his face.
In an instant ...
his manhood enters my tight, sweet place.
We elevate to a higher space.
Becoming one,
our souls dancing in place
to the beat of our own drum.
Until we fall asleep, exhausted.
We're done.
Woke up a few hours later,
to the rising sun.

Truth or Dare

He was unique.
A man of his mystique caught my eye
with his deep voice,
beautiful teeth,
and thick thighs.
We've worked together for some time,
and when he looked my way, I froze inside.
I was manipulated by his sleepy eyes.
One night,
we were working late – just him and I.
We couldn't resist the sexual tension
and strong vibes we felt exploding inside.
He looked at me and said,
"Let's play truth or dare."
I was game, and I chose dare.
He said, "I dare you to step up on this chair,
onto the desk with no underwear
while keeping your stilettos on."
I looked at him and said,
"No sweat."
This game got sexy real fast.
I walked over to him,
bending over to give him a lap dance.
Took his strong hands,
sliding them up my pretty dress.

As he removed my G-string real slow,
he couldn't resist
touching lady thick lips below.
He held my hand
as I stepped on the chair,
then up on the desk I go,
with my stilettos on.
As he stared, I said,
"Truth or dare?"
He said, "Truth."
What, are you scared to do a dare?
OK.
Then the questions flowed.
Are you attracted to me?
Yes!
Do I make you stiff?
Yes!
Would you like to join me on this desk
and tongue kiss my wet lips?
Oh hell yeah!!!
I smiled and said,
"I dare you to."
"But wait, I chose truth."
I know,
but these are my rules,
and after three questions of truth
you must dare to do
the last one you said yes to.

He licked his lips,
massaging his stiffness,
walks over to the desk
and spreads my legs apart.
Turns me upside down
and tongue bangs me
literally
on top of his work desk.
This was the sexiness you see in movies.
One more question after we screwed.
"Do I get a raise now?"
He looked at me
and started laughing out loud.
HELL YESSS!!!

Monday Morning

I met him in the club one night.
Head cocked to one side,
he motioned me to come sit beside him.
I looked,
gave him the side eye.
But intrigued by his mystique,
I glided by
with a supermodel strut.
Heels high,
and mini sundress on
that caught his eye.
I was fly!
And so was this guy.
As he held my hand,
I felt the electric vibe
tingling in between my thighs
and down my spine.
Just like his rise
fireworks went off inside.
The smile on his face
let me know our minds
were in the same place.
I gave him my number,
he called the next day.
In about an hour, I was at his place.
Being a bad girl

I was getting spanked
by his love stick,
and I loved the length.
He had me in positions
I was very comfortable with.
And his width
was extremely pleasing to me.
I cried out loud,
"Oh please, go deep!"
And deep he went.
He pulled me close aggressively
with his strong hands.
Kissing me around the neck,
his teeth pulled at my breast.
Magnetized to the 10th degree,
we puffed on the chief.
He knew exactly how to please me,
and as I pleasured him in every way,
the look on his face gave it away.
Trying not to hurt him that day
I knew this love affair would continue.
We fell asleep.
Silence.
Not a peep.
Woke up in the wee hours of the night
with such an insatiable appetite.
He's lying behind me,
slowly grinding.

His love snake slithering,
twisting inside of me,
I was moist in that special place.
We made love all night,
until the sunlight hit our faces.
We did this again and again
for the rest of the weekend
Until we woke up with squinting eyes,
just to realize,
it was Monday morning.

Pain

Why?

Pop-pop!
I drop.
Silence in the wind.
I cry.
Tears streaming down my eyes.
And I scream ...
WHY must another man die?
Why shoot 2, 3, 4, or 5 times?
Why do you not hear my cry?
Why does such evil live inside you?
Why do I threaten you?
Why can't I just be me?
Why are we harassed for just walking down the street?
Why are we so blind we can't see
good instead of bad when it pertains to black?
This is really sad.
Why, since the beginning of time,
have we been brainwashed to see all things black
in a negative light?
It isn't right!
Why must we fight for our lives?
Why all the anger inside?
Why do you not feel pride for your fellow brother
of another color?
Aren't we all the same inside?
Why do you feel more supreme than I?

You're not God.
We're all free.
At least that's what they want us to believe.
If all lives matter,
why are guns always drawn on me?
Shoot to kill.
Pop-pop!
I drop.
Silence in the wind.
Why am I unarmed, but you're still scared of me?
Why are my arms raised high
and yet the story you gave was still a lie?
Why do you have self-hate?
Shooting innocent people is a self-hate trait.
Why do you feel a need to demolish me?
Is this a part of your civil duty?
Why do you commit this crime,
but only get a slap on the hand?
Will someone please make me understand?
Why are our lives not valued?
We are human too, with families and dreams.
Why do you feel the need to shatter me?
I scream!
Pop-pop!
I drop.
Silence in the wind, they're at it again.
Why do I search for the truth
when I know it will never be revealed to me?
Why are we not free
when all we've done was help this country?

The Many Moods of a Woman

Why am I not free?
Why are there mental shackles on my feet?
Why am I not free?
Why do you think you're better than me?
Or is it that you want to be me?
Look like me.
Act like me.
Cornrow your hair and talk like me.
You even try to walk like me.
Does it hurt
that people who look like you are trying not to?
Is that why the monster awakens inside of you?
How dare I have pride.
Do I offend you because of my confidence?
Looking through your eyes,
you see me as arrogant.
Pop-pop!
I drop.
Silence in the wind.
There they go again.
Shooting another innocent Black man.
Black woman.
Our fathers.
Our mothers.
Our children.
I'm pleading to you again,
please stop!
No more pop-pop.
No more I drop.
No silence in the wind.

My hand to your hand,
let's drop the violence,
and stand side by side.
Stop the hatred.
Walk in silence.
Look me in my eyes and see my human side.
Before you pull that trigger, ask yourself,
would I want this to be my father?
My Mother?
My Sister?
My Brother?
Or my children?
You're the one with the weapon.
My hands are up.
There's no way you should feel threatened.
Just think for a second,
and reverse the scenario.
Would you want to be looking down
your own gun barrel?
Pop-pop!
You drop.
Silence in the wind.

A Brighter Day

Sitting here in my dark space.
Not reared by fear,
just a blank face.
I feel emptiness in abundance.
At times it's hard being me.
As I understand the underwhelming feeling
of drowning in nothingness,
loneliness, and unhappiness
in this stale ass relationship.
I am fed up and about to cry if I don't leave.
Too many responsibilities to just up and move,
so I'm trapped like an animal in a cage.
On the verge of snapping
at any given moment, time, or day
if he says one more phony ass thing to me.
Don't smile at me.
Don't send me off with a greeting in the morning.
I'm over it!
How can you just walk the walk
and think we're OK when we're not!
Time's up!
At this point there's only one thing I care about,
and that's our child.
She's the one who keeps me going,
keeps me motivated
and knowing there's a way out.

I can't continue to have her
in the midst of this unhappy household,
absorbing the vibes.
That's unnatural.
She's my number one priority.
As for you and I,
you know what's up.
At this point, I'm done arguing.
Not going to fuss.
I still love you,
but it's not enough.
Just taking it day by day as I must,
calculating the exit in time.
Don't act surprised
as if I pulled blindfolds over your eyes.
You know exactly how I feel.
I've told you a million times,
but you chose to continue to do nothing
and think I will have smiles for you in the morning.
No sir, I'm sorry.
I only show true feelings.
I do know one thing,
A brighter day is coming.

My Story

My story isn't new.
I'm a single mom struggling, just like you.
What can I do
but continue to rise and grow
into the woman I once knew,
who had it all figured out.
Until my dreams of being married,
with a beautiful child and a house
was derailed by the split from the one
I thought would be my spouse.
Tears stream down my face outlining my mouth.
What now? I think out loud.
Back against the wall, I slide down
meeting the ground.
Head buried deep between my knees
breathing heavily, loudly sobbing.
Thinking ...
I open my eyes, look up, studying the ceiling.
Eyes blinking.
As I wipe those tears away,
I look at my baby's sweet face.
Her eyes so full of life and grace.
Looking up to me, her Shero,
the one who's disappointed with her Hero.
As I continue to soak in my distress,
I look in the mirror and say,

"Sis, you're better than this."
I pull myself up,
managing a smile through the pain.
Heart beating off-beat, every day drains me.
Being a single mom was not a part of my life plan.
All my mommy friends, I hear you loud and clear,
and believe me, I understand.
At times being challenged by our sweet children,
having tantrums,
screaming out loud,
"MY HERO'S BETTER THAN YOU!"
As we hold our composure, we want to respond,
"Oh honey, if only you knew."
But we rise above
the inner struggles you don't see.
With grace, determination, and dignity,
my inner drive pulls me up
out of this depressive slump.
It's time to Rise Up!
Single Mommies, Rise Up!
Stop surviving
and start thriving in your own space.
Turning this rage of pain
into the strength of change, not shame.
At times, we're exhausted.
Always being the strong ones,
not blinking an eye.
But we don't have a choice
to just give up and be done.

The Many Moods of a Woman

So we push, and we push,
until the pushing's done.
But, is the pushing ever really done?
Using our pain and frustration
as the fuel we need for our reincarnation.
Changing and growing,
our energy flowing.
Dwindling.
And yet, we're transforming
these feelings into prosperity.
Rebuilding our confidence.
Restructuring until our anger has dissipated,
and our new selves elevated
into the sparkling diamonds
that shine brightly from the inside.
Breaking through the barriers
and the darkness on the outside.
Changing our lives,
one day at a time.
And we smile as our new selves arise.

To My Forever Love

My love:

It pains me to write this letter to you. Because every day of my life, you've been forever true. You had me at our first encounter, and my life was changed forever. An exciting ride just for you and I.

You had me mesmerized and on cloud 9 at the same time. On the flip side, we were like a roller coaster ride, toxic at times but all in all, we had a damn good time.

So, my heart breaks as I write this letter to you, because although you were good to me, I can't continue this love affair of what once was. In my true fashion, I have to move on.

My heart is broken into a thousand pieces, but as I'm on the floor picking up my shattered heart, I can't allow you to pull me back in with your romantic charm. I need to be real with myself this time, and break this forever bond. Things are just not the same, and it's time for me to move on.

As much as it pains me inside, you will always be my number one love. Please don't hold me any longer, or make this any harder. I need to soar high in the sky, like beautiful white doves, and close this chapter finally, ever after.

Please know I'll never forget you, and I will miss you. I'll keep these memories safe in my memory bank. Thank you for the greatest times, the lessons learned, the experiences many wished they could have known.

I was fortunate enough to have you in my arms. My love for you is strong as you embrace me with the temptations of our past. I know I've taken you for granted, but again, this cannot last.

It's hard for me to move on, but things must change. I must transform into my better self, and I can't do that with the memories of you holding me back.

So today, I release this dream of the past, and look forward to my future without your stronghold. You know I'm bold in my moves, and so are you.

I'll always cherish our history but today, I need to see myself clearly. I need to see what my full potential can be without the looming thoughts of, "What if?" or "What could have been."

I understand how many got lost in your abyss, almost losing their souls, while some not ever coming out of it. On the other side, however, to get them through the trying times, some used meditation and prayer, learning to maneuver and partner with you while remaining true to themselves.

It's still hard to believe you're no longer mine, but the angel and devil have played tug-of-war on my shoulders for the last time.

Although you have many names and ways of how others see you, there is still a mystery of intensity, an attraction so strong between us two.

But, I must let you go.

I'm closing this chapter because it needs to be released.

Thanks again for the lasting memories and our beautiful history.

To my Forever Love, affectionately known, as The Music Industry.

The Many Moods of a Woman

I am you and you are me.
Our lives together, intertwining.
Growing, flowing, getting stuck in life knowing
we're meant to head in an upward direction.
Off to the races with no regrets,
stopping to smell the roses
to see where life takes us.
Make us, break us,
turn us inside out to shake us,
we are women of many moods.
Layers upon layers
they sometimes mistake us.
Refusing to choose ourselves, at times,
while giving others our helping hands, no lie.
Putting their needs in front of our own,
we break down crying,
because we are broken on the inside
from the traumas we've dealt with in our lifetime.
Lonely on the outside,
we yearn for a significant other
to be our friend or maybe our lover,
or just simply be present
in the moment for each other.
There are many moods of a woman to uncover.
Constantly pushing forward to be financially free,
we pour love into our children,
celebrating their milestones, and nurturing.
Forgiving our enemies and
intellectually growing

into the butterflies we don't recognize
until we truly open our eyes
and see the rebirth of us for the first time.
Like a flower blooming,
our petals slowly open over time.
We're unknowingly flourishing and glowing.
We're thriving, getting wiser,
and showing up for each other.
Keeping the past in the past
as we continue to move forward.
Enjoying the journey, there's no time for complaining
or toxic raining on this parade.
We are fearless, beautiful, confident, and brave.
Sensual, sexy, passionate, no shade.
I'm a woman with many moods.
The many moods of a woman
translates to our individual grooves.
I'm a mother, sister, daughter, lover,
wife, friend, mistress uncovered.
I'm a woman with a plan.
At times you may not understand me
or my demands.
Unpredictable, I don't pretend while
moving strategically through life.
I'm a force to be reckoned with.
I am the light!
So, you may want to think twice
when approaching me.
I'm driven and focused
when it comes to my dreams

The Many Moods of a Woman

and accomplishing great things.
This is our journey,
moving and transforming without a clue
into who we are becoming.
Every day we put our best foot forward,
learning from our past mistakes.
True lessons without transgressions
only questions with each complicated layer
unraveling who we truly are at the core.
We are illuminating,
elevating ourselves.
With each step revealing our true selves
with no regrets.
Our mystique is appealing and uncommon,
representing
The Many Moods of a Woman.

Acknowledgements

My longtime dream has finally come true! I am extremely excited to share my book debut with you, a collection of poetic prose entitled *The Many Moods of a Woman*. It took me a while to get here, but I am here now and my journey would not have been complete without some amazing champions in my life who saw the progress unfold and blossom.

As I was going through this amazing journey of writing my first book, my family and friends were very supportive during this entire process. I would like to acknowledge those who were instrumental in pushing this project forward.

First, to my daughter, Zoë. My world is so much brighter with you in it. Thank you for inspiring me everyday. I see life differently through your eyes and you motivate me to keep moving forward to achieve my goals for us.

To my parents, Barbara and Darrell Sr., thank you for always supporting me. No matter how out of the box you think my ideas are, you are always there rooting me on.

To my siblings, Darrell II, Ebony, and Cecil and their families, you guys are the best! Thank you for always showing love and support no matter what.

Myron Spaulding, thank you for being supportive; I appreciate you.

Rhonda Dennis, you are more than my aunt, you are also one of my dearest friends. I thank you for always listening and inspiring me; I appreciate your honesty.

To my entire family, thank you for your unconditional love and support.

I truly believe there are people who come into your life for a season, and there are the gems who are here for a lifetime. I am fortunate to have a special tribe of friends for a lifetime who have become my extended family.

Dave Dickinson, from the time I was 18 years old, you always pushed my creativity to the next level. Thank you for always being in my corner and being real and honest with me every step of the way.

Jwaundace Candace, my sister-friend until the end. Thank you for always keeping me accountable and being the most supportive friend ever.

Nikki Skies, thank you for reviewing my work early on and encouraging me to move forward.

Andre and Lisa Fuller, I appreciate you for taking time out of your extremely busy schedules to share knowledge and valuable advice. I learn so much from you both.

To Rochad Holiday, I appreciate our conversations so much. Thank you for keeping me on track and making me see things in a different light.

Phill Branch, you inspire me in so many ways to step out of my comfort zone and keep pushing forward to accomplish my goals no matter what.

Darnell Gamble, you are a true light that shines so bright. Thank you for always being such an amazing and supportive friend.

Daylene Carter, I appreciate our pow wow sessions. Thank you for helping me take this project to the next level.

Marilyn Green, you have inspired me more than you know. Thanks for being truly you, and always keeping it real with me.

Sandi Robinson, you are more than a friend, you're also my big sister. Thank you for your professional guidance and showing great support throughout the years.

Scott Gordon, my brother from another mother, thank you for helping me find the last piece of the puzzle in order to finalize this book. You are a lifesaver.

Andrew Evans, my friend to the end, thank you for always helping me push my creativity forward.

Denice D. Richards, I could not have finished this book without you. You have come in and helped my vision come alive! You are the best collaborator and editor a girl could ask for, and also my newest friend for life.

I am so blessed to have such amazing people in my life. I love each of you and appreciate the time and support you have shown me throughout this process. Thank you for always being straight up and honest with me no matter what! I love all of you to the moon and back.

About Evette T. Fergerson

Evette T. Fergerson is an author and entrepreneur, a natural-born risktaker who lives life boldly and passionately. Her love for adrenaline, storytelling, and creative expression fuels her poetic stories, and challenges her to live out loud. Writing allows her to transform life experiences into powerful messages that inspire others.

Day-to-day, Evette wears many hats, including being a devoted mother to her daughter, Zoë, an entrepreneur, and fearless creative visionary who constantly pushes herself beyond her comfort zone. These intentional challenges have shaped an extraordinary journey of growth, courage, and reinvention.

Evette's career in media started as a college freshman at Grambling State University, where she became an on-air personality for the campus station KGRM. This experience sparked her path on radio. Throughout her college years and beyond, she worked for several stations and broadcast companies, including her internship with Stevie Wonder's radio station KJLH (Inglewood, CA), Personal Achievement Radio, Bailey Broadcasting (Los Angeles, California), KRVV-FM and KYEA-FM (Monroe, Louisiana), giving her a deeper appreciation for the business side of media and entertainment.

She eventually broadened her skills even more through an internship with Capitol Records, gaining invaluable industry experience she would carry over with her work in the music industry at Qwest/Warner Bros. Records with the late, great Quincy Jones and Elektra Entertainment. She later became a publicist for The Courtney Barnes Group, a leading Hollywood public relations firm representing top musical and television artists.

Entrepreneurship has always been at Evette's core and taken what she learned from the music industry coupled with her love for people, today her latest ventures were designed to inspire, educate, and elevate others.

Evette is the founder of The Artistic Voice Foundation, a nonprofit dedicated to empowerment, healing, and community impact through the arts. She is also the creator of The Artistic Voice Speakers Agency, representing art and entertainment-driven, inspirational, and storytelling speakers for audiences around the world. Additionally, Evette leads The Speakers Launch Lab, a development and coaching program for emerging and aspiring speakers who want to build confidence, craft their message, and turn their voice into a business.

As an author, *The Many Moods of a Woman* is her debut into the literary world and she is currently working on her next book, *The Triple "R" Factor: Reset, Restart, Reclaim Your Life While Finding Your Inner Voice*. Her writing reflects her belief in resilience, reinvention, personal growth, and transformation.

Evette lives by her mantra, "If I can skydive, I can do anything."

Energized by new experiences and teachable moments, she is "The Spark of Change," a woman dedicated to helping others break barriers, find their voice, and elevate their lives. She believes we are all meant to live boldly, dream freely, and step with courage into our greatest potential to live out loud.

To learn more visit evettefergerson.com or
tavspeakers.com

To send your thoughts and comments
about the book, email:
info@theartisticvoice.com

www.ingramcontent.com/pod-product-compliance
Lightning Source LLC
Chambersburg PA
CBHW051324120626
46547CB00015B/2384